AF493070

WHITE
Rum
AND
COCONUT
WATER

Poems by Natalie Corthésy

IAN RANDLE PUBLISHERS

Kingston • Miami

www.ianrandlepublishers.com

First published in Jamaica, 2023 by
Ian Randle Publishers
16 Herb McKenley Drive
Box 686
Kingston 6
www.ianrandlepublishers.com

ISBN: 978-976-8286-89-5

**A record of the Cataloguing-in-Publication Data information
is available in National Library of Jamaica**

Book design by Ian Randle Publishers
Cover design by CHILLCREATE Studio
Illustration by Teresa Fryxell
Author's portrait photograph by Eddie Otchere

Printed and bound in the United States of America

Cheers!

peenie wallies blink
what the flick is this green light?
happiness I think

CONTENTS

I.   White

cotton tree so high
hungry ground chews feet below
shade me when I die

Livity

Cherish the silent morning aching to laugh,
like a school girl longing to abandon the rules.
Beneath tender skin and frail apologies a callous heart hums.

Laughter is nothing more than a wolf's cry
a prelude to tears. There is no shame in
loving like a bull in a pen that can't get out.

But pride is a ring game of indifference for bullies.
Awakening to a bosom betrayed, day must cheat night
this burning star must dim her light to inspire devotion.

When skies comb melancholy clouds
a constant sun will braid joyful ribbons of gold
into the strands of dusk.

A promise of a carefree tomorrow
playful and fey. Troubled times become a neutered memory
replaced by vulnerable thoughts and a safe space to dream.

Faced with doubt, it is not enough to be resilient.
Dystopian landscapes must be reimagined.
Livity is an embrace of hope that renews every dawn.

Natty on the front line

"Broomy! Cobweb broom! Yaaad broom!"
signals the arrival of I and I, Jah Rastafari
ever living, ever faithful, never fear
the red, green and gold cotton crown
spiraled around my dreadlocks hair.

I pedal past the Yellow Bird Bar majestically,
khaki caftan flapping like a Nyabinghi drum break.
The brooms on my shoulder are heavy,
a symbol of spiritual livity conquering Babylon's mind-quake.

Pants length tucked in my socks
perspiration fueled my thirst for river baths
and the taste of an irie daughter's lips.
If only this kind of sweetness was wholesale.
Advertised on shop walls painted magenta, selling sweet sips:
"Bag juice sold here. Twenty-five dollars. Right here."

What people really want is chicken foot, chicken back, and turkey neck.
If I sold a broom for all the foreign women on the beach
who wanted my ital and my chalice
I and I would be rich, not kicking after brown mongrel dogs
chasing my bicycle downhill with malice.

New broom sweep clean, but old broom know the corners.
You can't sweep bad mind from a dirty heart,
even if you buy, borrow, or beg the broom;
or balance it on your head from Heroes Circle to Megga Mart.

Natalie Corthésy

It is not Miss Constant Spring fault.
She was not taught to look up.
Now she lives uptown she can't remember being black.
So when she sees Rasta coming, she flags me down and asks:
"If the broom can't reach my roof, can I get my money back?"

I am really selling over-standing, an ideology of cleanliness
that transcends political art and historical artifacts.
On the frontline of negritude,
the more Rasta advances, the more Babylon extracts.

Yardies

Kingston city's intersections are littered
with angry boys   faces
crushed like old newspaper
too torn to read   crumpled dreams
written into their expressions with bold print.

You can't just show up and start
begging   windscreen wiping is a career
for professional idlers and yardies
in training   not laggards.
Credentials are no joke.

Don't know your father   boom!
Mother beat you with electric cord
brap!   Held a gun before you were ten
bouy!   Bellyful of rage
yet you're hungry   bloodoy!

Steal or take   a wiper and a rag.
Fill a used plastic bottle with soap.
find the Don   who controls the corner.
Respect is payable in advance.
A little herb might improve your chance.

Shoeless feet blistering on
smoldering concrete   zigzagging
through traffic jammed roads.
Rapping on frozen glass for change
is a man-making vocation.

      Natalie Corthésy

You have to want to   kill your father
to save your mother   and leave your mother
to save yourself.   Throw your pride down
on the yellow brick curb
upturned fingers huddled in supplication.

God's providence is a cracked window
Babylon can slip coins through
without touching   sullied hands
that have forgotten unblemished memories
of milk filled breasts and cradling arms.

The odor of spirits wilting in the sun
waiting to be seen   conjures up
a vision of speckled ripe bananas   ignored
for too long.

Talented woman

The distance from country to uptown is eighty years,
a sixty year wedding anniversary, two children in wedlock,
a few bastard children and some talent.

First she has to outshine her siblings,
forgive her uncle and outrun the village ram.
This takes courage in a rural village where the walk for water is nine miles,
animals must be reared for food and there is a single pit latrine.

Sometimes the journey must be taken with mismatched shoes,
with nothing more than a navel orange in her pocket
and a banana leaf to cover her head from September's downpour.

The raw will tightening in her belly is like the hunger of a mangy dog.
She can wash, cook, clean, feed the hogs, walk to school,
carry water on her head up hill to the house many times,
all in one day.

Selling suck-suck for pocket money is not enough.
She needs a relative in town to take her in.
She will have to wash, cook and clean some more in exchange for room
and then find a part time job so she can save the college fee.

She must use all her talent to find a husband
who sees her blooming in the weeds.
From this crucial move, all others will be choppy or placid.
She must jump through macca to find hope on the hill.

Natalie Corthésy

Neville's curry goat joint

This is no ordinary cook shop.
Built on the country roadside of nobody's land
brightly painted orange and green
so everybody will want to stop.

Brown man can get mannish water
before he gives the pretty royal a ride
and also carry home curry to town
for his mistress, wife and daughter.

Policemen order the special after eventful speed traps.
A large box with white rice, boiled green bananas,
and raw veg on the side. Paired with a cup of broth,
after you eat, you are sure to collapse.

Aunty so and so is always finding fault.
She complains to Miss Pepsi who runs the bar.
She wants to add a chicken wing to her goat,
extra gravy and one bag of salt.

Neville, the owner, is also the chef.
When the cook shop is corked with people
and Neville starts to get cross,
Pepsi simply cut her eye and pretend she is deaf!

Barrel baby

Everybody inna di yard know seh
mi baby fadda tek up residence inna one bus shed.
Him pitch living room pon di side walk wid rock stone divan
and build up newspaper mattress wid cardboard bedhead.

Him closer to Jesus now wid the church yard behind di wall.
Babylon don't see he is the sermon,
wid Judas billboard ova him head –
"100 great reasons 100 suite experiences"
as if him life worth nothing at all.

You know seh tings nah run right.
Aunty Dimples send di barrel from foreign
and all mi get is cornflakes, detergent, one bag a second hand clothes
and a white dolly dat cyaaan share without a fight.

Whappen to the school shoes dem
and di Fucci bag fi go a dance?
How she expec mi fi get a new baby fadda if mi look bruk
and mi ragga ragga pickney dem a advertise mi economic circumstance?

Is not me one poor if poor people cyaaan eat.
Big house up town wid grill-up grill-up and bad dawg
don't mean seh gun man a sleep.
We cyaaan depend pon barrel fi keep poor people off di street.

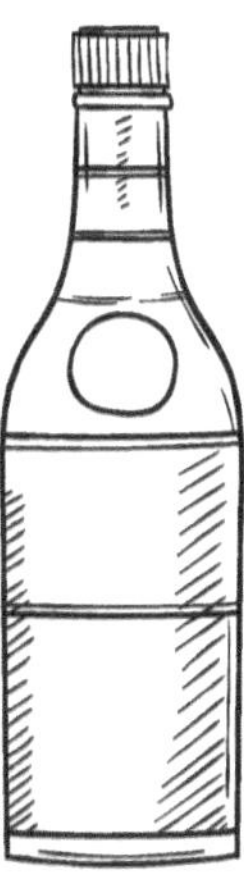

II. Rum

juicy mango sky
cloud whistles a fruity song
I bite in and fly

Summer came in December

Father's voice invoked famine until hunger overflowed.
Lately, his empty words dangled like sour mangoes in the yard
the kind only a brave child would dare to devour
taking the entire seed into a wide open mouth.
I hid my laughter behind smiling eyes and silence.
Fear of his terror swallowed my courage.
His indifference transposed my shame into acceptance.

My father's box

Filled with vinyl albums - Marley, Fela, Santana, Mingus,
instead of hugs. I struggle to digitize his analogue goodbye
and reboot my memory of the son I have been.

My eyes dance in tears
like ice cubes melting in his white rum and coconut water.
I don't want to remember the temper
that launched dinner through the window on to wilted hibiscus blooms.
The seat at the head of the table is empty.

I am learning to pack away emotions in right angles
and translate belonging from antiques.
Strange to find more tenderness shrink wrapped around records
than in the sleeves of my retrofitted heart.

Love is captured land you have to slash and burn
for sugar cane to prosper.
But my despondence is a rusty machette
too heavy to wield and too dull to dig.

Surely a childhood colonized by songs
of not being good enough can be liberated
by a box of blues, not the open palm kind
he would smash across a cheek, fingers stacked with rhythm.

Like a ponciana bleeding crimson to camouflage its exposed roots,
I am my father's son; even if I never chose my name.
Rather than sit in the shade of doubt,
longing for, longing to be outside the box,

I should have asked him
"teach me how to ride a bike" or
"how do I pick ackees from their husks".
Knowledge of this kind of danger is not engraved on the dermis
like the risk of becoming my father.

Polished wife

Don't look. Listen.
I am sleeping inside
a ceiba tree with a ram goat tied to its trunk,
dreaming I am a double skinned drum.

Eager to be the dream catcher
I dare to move up from here.
Drifting through emotional storms and lightning tongues,
I rise.

Limbs lifting husband,
roots feeding children until my branches bend.
Austerity imbues me until I become
the drummer and the strummed.

Nobody sees me as the polished wife
who outgrew her forest,
nor the goat as my companion
with whom I am evenly yoked.

Everyone wants to be buried at my feet
shelter unfurled, memories etched in the bark of my skin.
I am a brand new second hand bass
wailing, heavy rhythm exhaling into the ear.

Natalie Corthésy

Add some water to your rum

An average man tries to chase a great woman
by watering her down
like adding water to your drink when you are feeling tipsy.

Tells her she laughs too loud, or not enough
asks her to change from red rum to white
knowing she is the fever grass and sugar cane in his Trelawny Mist.

So he keeps pouring
love-drunk and emotionally vapid.
"that dunce dog doesn't know what he's doing."

Period

Turning the light off in my slumbering

verse   left the page pregnant

with silences and dog ears.

A dim view of words

eclipsed   by solitude and unrest.

Clipped like a paper doll

tabs   snipped and scattered

I have nothing to say.

Soon come

I am afraid to say what I feel
Befuddled by the notion of loving
unloving, longing, belonging,
tender and tendered feelings.

When will you hold me close?
The chapter of your boyhood is closed.
Start over. Rip the pages from the spine.
Begin again. Happiness is overdue.

I feel like I am wasting time
accidental girl punctuating your timeline.
Ten minutes hot, two days slow.
Ten minutes hotter, two days no show.

I want a love that is good.
The kind of goodness you can knead with your own hands
like dumplings with a secret ingredient
you secretly lick your fingers after each bite.

Easier to believe in self-reliance
than rely on love's tattered eaves
Nailed into place above a frail heart
where my one drop heartbeat drums

I peer into his floating metal face.
Eyes flicker unlocking the facade
of infinite dreams trapped in a box.
Voiceless ideas boxing about his mind

What I really need is balance.
Centre is a shade of blue balancing the rim.
I want to learn to paint it from memory
but I cannot unlearn deception

So I tell myself "soon come".
Respect, devotion, love, all coming
from his eyes, in his smile, out of the box.
Sea blue, Sky blue, bluebell smiling.

Natalie Corthésy

III. And

shame so sharply stings
wait and see can't change the dance
twirl my spirit wings

Before I go

I am ready to die.
I closed my bank accounts and cancelled my insurance.
I selected a photograph of myself from my other life for the
     funeral programme.
I was young and virile then.

I rummaged through the random things I collected for years that
     served no apparent purpose.
I discovered a silver pen that was given to me as a long service
     award,
three flashlights and a mitt to clean my Italian leather shoes.

I laughed with my cousin on the veranda as we sipped sorrel
and gazed out at Kingston's verdant hillside
adorned with red Poinciana blooms and garlands of yellow
     mangoes.

I want to be buried next to my uncle in the cemetery downtown.
The family plot behind the Baptist church in the rural village
where I grew up is no resting place.

How the memories of walking eight miles to and from school,
feeding the hogs, tying out the donkey and
being whipped for drinking an entire tin of condensed milk still
     haunt me.
I am sure to meet only slave ancestors in the afterlife if I return
     there.

I hugged my grandsons and reminded them to take care of each
        other.
Despite being petrified of my dentures and horrified that I ceased
        to wear them,
they allowed me to tuck them into bed and kiss them goodnight.

In my last conversation with my daughter,
I sat quietly and listened to her judgement of my shortcomings as
        a father.
This unexpected confession of resentment took decades
to pick its way through her clenched teeth that chewed lies as
        she smiled.

She was right.
You can only give what you have inside,
nothing more.
Had I given so little that no one would remember me?

When I kissed my wife goodbye and handed her the photograph,
I was overcome with desire to be desired
by the one person to whom I was already dead.

There was too much neglect,
too many women, and children with other women,
for my "I love you" peace offering to fit in her emaciated bitter
        heart.
Somehow she flourished despite her refusal to acknowledge that
        I gave her status.

At the door,
I turned away and stumbled
into the unknown, chastened and repentant.

                                                    Natalie Corthésy

April's curtain call

I am the last guava left on the tree,
a lopsided stage hacked mid trunk.
The missing branches turned firewood are smoking
someone's heaven on top and hell below
but the cornmeal pone in the middle will not bless my soul.

The birds have pecked and pecked and pecked
racing worms to a pulpy centre
where my sweet perfume masks decay and the lament of my seedy core.
I will not be handpicked for jam or flaky tarts.
I will not be stoned by children, nor slightly bruised before being bitten
    blissfully.

The sun shined my skin for weeks
until I was a reflection of her golden globe.
The rain wept with me, lightly
kissing droplets on my withering cheeks.
Now I stand alone patiently waiting for applause.

My own roots will shake me from this limb
and cast me to the ground into a crowd of ants.
Soldiers will retrieve my remains to nourish one of their own;
Queens are not born
they are made.

If clay is willing and nature is kind,
memories of me shall channel through the earth
to nascent stems and lime green leaves to nurse a seedling.
I am last in death and first in life;
the fruit and the tree dancing in the garden pantomime.

Threshold

"Patience in life,
Patience in death", the saying goes.

So I wait for a window to open or a door to close
but my grief is a house without an exit.

I never understood the urgency of living
until its flickering went out

like the last breath of
midnight, midnight, midnight.

Bang

You were born to soar
through recycled hearts,
and into my song.

What brought you here
is not the reason you stayed.
You are a bird on a limb,

waiting
for bullets to ring out
and the flock to give chase.

You glide towards me
fearless and exposed.
Click, click, click.

The gun reloads and takes aim
You plummet from the sky
like a jelly coconut

bellyful of living water and joy.
A deafening air of peace
swiftly silences our choir.

Sweet Mandora boy
I love you more
more than I did the day before.

Wake

let the moonlight curl her fingers
into my sun kissed hair
feather on her tongue
muting beginnings and swallowing endings
repeat after me
"I am loved"
luminescent strands orbit my desire
to be blue   and blackened with regret
I lean into her   the darkling swells
into willful denial
I think I died again

what I tell myself when I forget
I don't love you anymore

you are a gift
and you have gifted me many things
memories   and a hope that love brings.

I lost count of the kisses
and playful words   fleeting
like Jamaican mango hummingbirds.

to another   who receives you
with open self   transcending your grief
filling your shelf   with new things and neutered memory.

erasing the playful words and kisses
with love's emery   my wings were pared
so I could not follow.

my tongue was parched
but I could not swallow the pain
your gift springs.

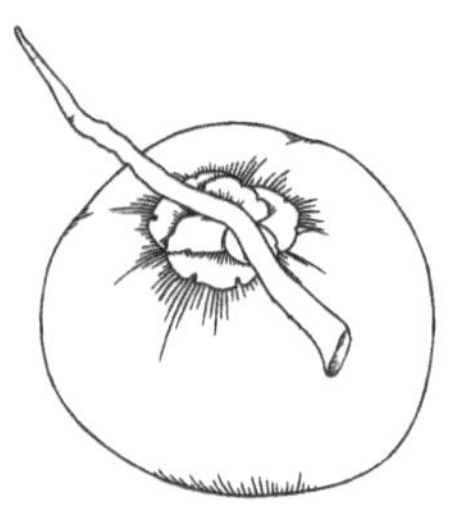

IV. Coconut

fat girl really loves cakes
sadness is best slice by slice
icing hides mistakes

Miss Jamaica

Her inner-city is not a papier maché of zinc sheets
or narrow streets lined with sisters braiding each other's hair.
It's a state of mind for urban outcasts.
A mental journey she takes. Marooned.
The choice she makes not to smoke weed at ten
or refuse to take hood at eleven.

She inherited buildings of self-hatred twelve stories high.
No playgrounds. No gardens.
A ginger lily can't grow in concrete.
How many beatings will it take to convert her body into street art?
Electric cables bridge light into the tenement scheme
but the dusk of poverty veils everything in sight.

Her spirit is chastened, yet her mind is feral.
The mongrel barks.
The thief passes.
She is toothless and Babylon's long bag is empty.
If only she could change the narrative in the yard
by pissing on the gate column with disregard.

The thief can work his way out or die his way out.
The same blade of hunger that sticks goat sticks sheep.
Real starvation is deep, concealed
by the domino game on the corner
and the church-bar-school sandwiches
littered through parishes at every mile post.

Maybe the ritual of dance hall is more powerful than obeah,
and the initiation of a thirteen year old shotta cheaper than a
    meal deal.
Miss Jamaica's inner-city throbs to the pulse of automatic
    machine guns.
She is nobody's daughter and she has buried her sons.
But no one can conquer her ghetto fortress.
She will not abdicate or love less. This queen reigns.

Natalie Corthésy

The me you cannot see

Bouncing off skin
gleaming from locks
Roughening the streets
I shine from within.

I paint unlit skies
and minor piano keys
I blend in with blues
dreaming cage bird flies.

I am not humour.
I am not magic.
I am not death.
I am not a hole.

I shine not burn

I don't care what they call me

I am not a boy anymore. But I still like being tucked in
I don't really understand why people are obsessed with the
    colour of my skin.
In the school yard they call me "plantation owner"
because my hair is not stacked like peppercorn and
my patois cannot disguise my residential area code.

I am not yet a man. But I am not ready to be one.
Why the hurry to define children who just want to have fun.
On the playground they call me "batty boy"
because I am polite, I won't fight and I don't enjoy
watching porn huddled over a cell phone screen.

I am not a good son. But I am trying to be
Everybody says I look like my father but I don't agree.
At family dinners they call me "mommy's hand bag"
because I would sit on her lap, rest my chin on her bosom
and smile until her eyes glistened back at me like naseberry
    seeds.

I am not an unwilling friend. But I enjoy being an island.
My people are the people that have no people, no brand.
At camp they call me "Zero" because I refused to choose a
    nickname
I think they got it right though. I am open and closed,
I am all and nothing, complete on my own, filled with infinite
    potential.

I am a believer. But my faith is knottily founded on mystery

         Natalie Corthésy

Maybe god has chosen my name and wants me to rewrite history.
In church they call me "sonny boy" because I challenged the
    Trinity.
Funny how my testimonial about forgiveness irked the
    congregation
All I know is, no matter what you are called, always answer back.

2,000 acres of Paradise

What would you do with my bad feelings
if I gave them to you,
if I told you I was drowning?

Would you hold out your hand to take mine,
or skip me down stream like a stone?
Would you listen to the gurgling

Sweet River that runs through my story
towards the Great House of delusion
I constructed with blocks of salt?

Will you offer me Plantation Paradise
rolling plains of shady banyan tress
with lianas that strangle the root of my misery?

A recessed portrait of a servile negro
hangs like faded tapestry in my ancestral gallery.
I have become my own captive, yet I cannot master myself.

Slavery's wrath has watered me down
and left a hint of rum in my salvation.
Dew cannot fill what rain has left empty.

I want to swim in laughter and float in tears
to be drunk with feelings of belonging
purposefully adrift, and buoyant with liberation.

Natalie Corthésy

Lament

God love me

From the day my mother was forced ripe by the Don
A constant gardener of little girls
planting bad seed in every yard
but fathering no one.

To the day I was left
on the hospital steps when I was born.
No angels came with milk and honey
for the child who bears his mother's scorn.

On the day the reapers left me
in a factory for discarded youth to rot
I cried out for mercy "God love me"
I am the homeless bird that you forgot.

When the day swallowed me whole
and night smothered me with persistent poverty.
The aunty beat, the pastor lied, the gardener stole,
I was everybody's property.

All the days the gun strapped to my ankle
like a third foot stalking innocent lives.
The aunty cried, the pastor prayed, the gardener died,
I am the wretch who survives.

Until the day I found my way
through the labyrinth of zinc fence around my shame.
Slashed and burned the wrath
that camouflaged my path and sullied my name.

God love me, love me now.

Landscaping

help isn't coming
motherhood has made me slovenly
loving has wilted the bougainvillea blooms
guarding the walls of my spirit garden
I am scratched up and incomplete

motherhood has made me slovenly
am I not worth saving from weeds
netting through good soil and stone
I long to be the bird god feeds
sinner, savior, salvation requires wings

am I not worth saving from weeds
waiting in my fatherless marriage
ploughing blade of grass tickles then stings
and new birth mirrors still life
with one eye open smiling back at me

waiting in a fatherless marriage
shame germinates in memories
buried in my unkempt bed of dreams
I forgot to water the seedlings
still they flourish on self-hatred

shame germinates in memories
beneath fallen hibiscus petals
blushing at my nakedness and scars
silence muffles my children's screams
help isn't coming

Natalie Corthésy

V.   Water

rainy nights come quick
pump pum bush blooms in warm thighs
strike lightning dick!

Casting rod

bathe me in salt
give me a sip of the water calling
the fisherman by the shore

cast me a line and let it drift
I want to take the hook in my mouth

love is a sacrifice of endless sea
ocean and sand holding hands
for as far as one can see

when I ask for tenderness
give me sunlight
and palmfuls of warm breeze

pressing against my shoulders
then slowly down my spine

immerse me in this tide
of loving and being loved in return
reel me into you

Relic

The torque in my chest stopped.

An unfamiliar stillness replaced the pounding
as its echo dropped.

The tin box that guards my gilded memories
is a cursed gift, my only treasure.
The pirates have come and gone. The slavers too.

"Man, is man, is man".

Undaunted, the bricoleur takes pleasure
collecting fear and loss from the mechanical carcass.

Oiling dreams, fueling our fate.
Toiling through trials
transforming this timeless thing.

Slowly yet fast, fiercely though tender.

A peculiarly ornate but whimsically simple cocoon
beautifully reimagined.

Fluttering returns,
breaking the curse of tragedy archived in my body,
filling me up with celebration.

I swoon into the bricoleur's hands
and emerge from love's tyranny
like a Monarch draped in silk

metamorphosed and sentient.

Natalie Corthésy

My girl

I want to make room for you
in my mother's house,
next to me when our children rise
inside the sheath of my affection
on my solitary beach of salt and light
by my side at the river
where I graze but still find no water
I will follow you and find rest.

One by one I remove the weeds in my garden
that do not want you to bloom.
I prepare a place to lay our heads
a home that is yours and mine
for a never ending summer of sunsets.
Kneel with me. Feast with me.
I won't leave you behind.
I'll make room.

One sip

Pour me out
Like you would condensed milk across a bowl of hominy
    porridge.
See, it is a golden orb of comfort.

Swallow my spiraling words until
I fill you up with reverie to the brim
sweetening your morning in mouthfuls.

Let us stir, make a warm memory
spooning, taking from the edge and blowing cool.
We feast with hungry eyes.

Wanting more than we can behold
love offers us just one sip.
So we clasp hands under the table.

Stagga back

"Excuse me Miss,
Miss fluffy tail...
...Miss goody,
Miss sweetie...

I wish you were stuck in my teeth
cavity deep and taking root.
A confectioner's wet dream
of sticky delight, hard on the palette.

Round coconut brown rhythm,
stagga back wine on my tongue
linger your ginger and lime while I suck.
You are just my size.

I want to fuck you without fear
or favour licky-licky girl.
Grease paper can't trap
Your sugar magic."

Catch

Toes press down on coarse black sand.
Impatient, wanting crashes in.
The wave breaks. Heart shells
towed under by a current of fear.

Foam bubbles slick burnt skin.
A consolation for the awkward feet
half buried but not taking root
almost lifting though wingless.

Promises flutter when plucked.
We replace them with feathered maybes
planing the surface of this love
drenched sea, brimming with salt and light.

Wait.
Wait for me.

Palms open reluctantly
like starfish tentacles
draped over polished stones
I cannot grasp without blistering.

Dazed by twilight humming
our silent chorus. Tongues scorched.
Scaled words are a fragile bait
tangled in a net meant for drifters.

Natalie Corthésy

Abandon slings through the August sky
flickering. Sun hook glints, dusking clouds
charry blue. I have been here before
lolloping at the shore.

Wait.
Wait for me.

Tipsy

my verse is scattered
words gather for tea at noon
lunch never mattered